The Thought Compendium
Poems by Dylan Russo

Email: dyrussomedia@gmail.com

Twitter: twitter.com/DylanRussoMedia

Facebook: facebook.com/DylanRussoMedia

Cover Artwork by Athira Sanal

Introduction

Welcome to "*The Thought Compendium*"

The poems within this book touch upon my thoughts, specifically observations about my existence, my behavior, and human nature. This poetry acted as my outlet for exploring deeper thoughts about the world around me and the role I play in it. Writing bestowed upon me the ability to encapsulate my thoughts in bubbles of words, so that I may keep them for future reflection. I strongly believe my writing has helped me to grow as a person in positive ways and I owe an immeasurable debt to it. I have cataloged in this compendium a portion of my own journey of growth. It is up to you to decide what you extrapolate from the text.

The Thought Compendium was intentionally designed to be a collection of thoughts on concepts I felt were more universally significant. I wanted to encourage both life and behavioral analysis with my poetry. My primary goal is to bring the reader to question not only their routine emotional patterns, but also their interactions with others by viewing others empathetically. Fear and anger are real prisons that restrain us to viewing our own lives and the lives of other people through a negative bias; a bias we ourselves cultivate and nurture. We play into the hands of our ego and develop a self-obsession that prevents us from truly connecting as human beings. We need to learn to escape our predispositions.

This is my effort to promote social objectivity and a healthy disconnection from the self. It is crucial to note that pure objectivity is not possible as we are not perfect creatures. The closest one can become to being truly objective is to accept and make an honest effort to understand opinions and concepts that originate outside of one's own predefined moral comfort zone. As long as you do not immediately reject the thoughts and ideas that do not align with your personal value system you can gain a more wholesome perspective of the world and people around you. Always strive to maintain an open mind and to withhold judgment.

The mind is a powerful tool and thoughts are vehicles we use to explore this great, enigmatic universe in which we exist. Through the power of thought we can analyze and understand our faults and make a serious effort to change for the better. Whether we grow as human beings or perpetuate our current social and emotional conditions is up to us as individuals. I want you to stop and reflect on things internally as well as externally for at least a few minutes every day. Free thought is essential for our growth, but proves to be a difficult task when we live so caught up in a fast-paced and despondent world suffocating on superficial negativity. Let us take a step back and learn to appreciate this beautiful world we are lucky to be able to experience.

I hope you enjoy the poetry,

Dylan Russo

Thought Bridges

I built you a thought bridge
So you could cross it
To be closer to my core
To the smallest parts of me
And become familiar

Every thought is an island
I've built houses on every one
And you've just begun discovering them
Bridge by bridge
We are getting closer
So close that I can feel it

We are transient
So come now while there is time
While you can see what I see
Before what I see is gone
Hurry across the thought bridges
And learn my true shape

I am dying geometry
But you can remember
The impressions I made

Karmic Threads

We are all bound by a thread called life
It's tied to me
It's tied to you
And everyone we will ever know
Connecting every living soul

We drag our threads through busy rooms
Only able to keep moving forward
One room at a time
Each room presenting a new obstacle
Which tests the integrity of our thread
Each room introduces to us new souls
With whom our threads will cross
They will become tangled
Permanently entwined into knots

These knots tell the story of our journey
Through the many rooms of our lives
Shaped by the moments
Shaped by our actions
Defining the connections we make
Forming bonds both good and bad
And each bond will be our map
Leading us into the next room
For better or for worse

At the end of my life
Should I be allowed to retrace my thread
I want to cherish
To be proud of the bonds I made
For others to be proud of bonds with me
And how in a single moment
We shaped the direction of each other's lives

Sonder

You are just another face in the crowd
Another actor in this play called life
Maybe I'll pass you on the street
Or I'll see you through a car window
Carrying on with your day
Enacting your individual routines and rituals
Visiting places I've visited before
In the company of other strangers
Who fulfill an important role for you
Affecting your life in ways I can't imagine

We won't find out how similar we are
If we would be great friends or enemies
Chances are we won't even exchange words
Existing in what seems like separate worlds
There is a chance you'll notice me
But then I'll fade into the background
And you'll forget me not long after
If you ever noticed me at all
To you, the all but invisible man
I am just another face in the crowd

Pessimism Personified

I'll make sure you remember me
My words are my tomb
Where I am trapped eternally
Pickled in the womb
A parasite hyperbole
Yearning to consume
The leaves upon the cherry tree
The glass will be half-empty

I am the pessimistic heathen
I am the demon
I'll tie anchors to your hopes
I'll make sure you stay weakened

Once you've felt my negativity
Your world view will be changed
I'll burrow deep and plant a seed
That will grow until the roots ingrain
And summon a sadness inside your brain

I am the pessimistic heathen
I am the reason
Why you'll never dream again
Why you seem so beaten
You'll never think a happy thought
As long as I'm still breathing

Shapeshifters

Behold the speed of an epiphany
The realization is quick
And before I know it
It has already passed
And I have changed

Change is perceived gradually
But it is a constantly occurring phenomenon
From each and every experience
A lesson can be drawn

When this lesson is observed
Suddenly I am something new
Similar to before
But different at the same time
I identified growth
For better or for worse
Happening second by second
Like clockwork

This is the journey of a shapeshifter
Inconsistent version
Unstable form
I learn what I am
Only to become different
Every time I recognize myself

Conversation Chemist

Talking to people is like mixing chemicals
Each word could be extremely volatile
You never know what kind of reaction you'll get
Eventually we learn patterns through experience
But there are still so many untested mixtures
Any one of them could ruin the concoction
Or transform the dynamic of your relationship
A master chemist can predict the result
But there is a large margin for error
Untested chemicals contain hidden properties
There are always variables you can't account for
So be careful with what you choose to say
It could blow up in your face

Capricious Truth

The sermon has been going on awhile
In the unstable church of my head
The voice reviews truth in denial
Unraveling the tightest thread
All the forms we see are fake
He speaks to raise me above the lie
But I will never really be awake
The world gouged out my mind's eye

I can't see anything for what it is
I can only speculate
And learn to designate
What I hold inside my fist

The truth I seek is ever-changing
Inconsistent at its best
The rules just keep rearranging
But my brain becomes obsessed
With futile attempts to understand
To know that which can't be known
But with every answer I demand
Another question has been grown

Certainty is a pipe dream
It can not be achieved
And so I believe
Real truth remains unseen

No Less

You are the artist, the creator
Truth is a product of your eyes
Whatever you find it to be

Oh, smith me the blade of reason
So I can commit treason against myself
Oh, smith me the shield of doubt
So I can reject the burn out preacher
I need no sermon
I need no crutch

My truth is no less than his truth
My art is no less than his art
My heart is no less

Finding The Right Words

My thoughts never stray far from the lexicon
Because if I'm going to say it
I don't want to say it wrong
There exists the exact right words for me to find
A handful of phrases waiting to be combined
To reach you
No, not really
To help you reach me
I just need to chose my words carefully

I will construct a sound bridge
To help you cross over
Every ocean of a mental glitch
I will tear down the wall that divides us
With the same rope I use to escape conversation ruts

This is my life preserver
The sword I forged in the eyes of the observer
Meant to offer up a slice of perspective
So keep your mind open and receptive

Yes, sometimes my words will fail us
Not every hopeful gamble
Can be backed by a royal flush
But it is a chance I will continue to take
Even if it means I must be as cunning as the snake
And deceive you
Into seeing things a new way
To put my vision on display
I will find the right words to say

My Crazy Thoughts

I have a predilection toward insanity
A detachment from reality
For it is the hammer I used
To break down the walls
Of my Sulkatorium

The wonder drug I ponder with
A vehicle for my thoughts
To reach farther destinations
Unbound from the many chains
That held my mind in place

If solid ground is what I seek
I have laid bread crumb memoria
To summon myself home
But I won't be afraid to explore
To defy the progenitor

He who exemplifies stagnation
Bearing a horde of new children
Each more complacent than the last
I will want for more than them
I will dream the dreams they can't

Imagination is my nationality
Language is my religion
For they do not give me the answers
But instead
The tools to ask the questions

Organic Donor

Death is a graduation
The great stepping stone
Goodbye world, hello universe
A transition of phases
Departing from a vessel and an identity
Existing as one with everything

I was built in the star furnace
A troupe member of the carbon cavalcade
Living in the Gaea kiln
Until my body melts and my atoms spill
And the colony that makes up my body
Parts ways

I will be recycled
But won't retain the self
I will not be I
But pieces of what I once was
Will take on new shapes
Form new bonds
Until the bio-product they make degrades
Just like I did
And will be re-purposed
Again and again

Eidolon

I must see beyond my impression
And escape the label of human pup
Rectify this old transgression
To get my neural networth up

I've always been standing by
Resident of the antechamber
They promised I could touch the sky
But looking has always been my nature

I pay tribute to the eidolon
For the first time in who knows how long
The toll is hefty
Though wagered against the worth
I count my blessings

I will heed his dogma
And continue my march on
With no fear of trauma
Guided by the eidolon

He who illuminates potential within me
And reassures my path with hope
He has granted me the key
To climb this upward slope

I am the eidolon
No god or king deserves my credit
To find where I belong
I assumed the role of medic
And healed a tired wound

Day By Day

Tomorrow I face the colossus
But my sword has seen better days
My courage has considerably weakened
And my motivation swiftly decays

Tomorrow is a faceless colossus
A massive and overwhelming foe
It fills me with a great and horrible fear
Of the things I don't yet know

Tomorrow is coming quickly
And its arrival has made me afraid
Yes, tomorrow is coming soon
But for now I have the rest of today

Today is a fight I can manage
Only time keeps the colossus at bay
But when the time comes I'll be ready
And maybe I'll be okay
When tomorrow becomes today

Balancing Act

I've got the consistency of a monsoon
Always changing like the moon
But I wane before I wax
Always waiting for the next relapse
Unable to relax before it happens
Unable to meet the challenge
The captain of a sinking ship
Where does one go to get a grip?
I'm ill-equipped to fight these monsters
I came but I didn't conquer
What if I can't get stronger than this?
And I can't subsist in the real world
What if I'm a fraud?
Who has been faking it all along
Prolonging my stay in the darkness
Trying to hit invisible targets
Or maybe I'm just an armless man
Who doesn't know how to follow plans
Sinking in the quicksand slowly
Before I fall out of the great oak tree
And get stuck on repeat mode
What if I'm more ebb than flow?
And I don't know balance
Living in an asymmetrical palace
Poisoning my own chalice in silence
Proliferating the virus
Campaigning a bias that's wrong for me
And I just can't see it's feeble
I need to make both sides equal

Fate

In the place where phantom constellations shine
We're on a winding road of lies
We're countless miles from the truth
What is it we think that we will find?
Can we reach the end?
Will we have to say goodbye?
A maze of stars is hollow
Through the eye of a looking glass
Blinking lights of unknown fate
Hidden by celestial masks
Is it something we can follow?
Will we be lost along the way?
We're nothing more than dust
We're shackled to the fray
If you can't dream are you alive?
We won't sleep until we die
Our hourglass is running out of sand
Life is finite
Time is falling through our hands
We are fleeting like shooting stars
Quickly blinking out of sight
We race across the sky
A simple moment is all we are
Eclipsed we flee like rays of light
Live today and die tonight

Troubled By Time

I am uncontrollably oozing numbers
That coagulate into a thick pool
My own personal fountain of youth

Cataloging every second that I spill
The hours add up quickly
Before too long I'll
Fade away with
The great
Flood

Time ticks tirelessly toward tomorrow

Now I'm like an old man
I've got a broken roof and it's raining
Sporting a defense of pots and tupperware
So desperate to catch a break
They fill faster than I can empty them
And the rain falls harder still

One day they are going to overflow
One day I'll be in over my head

You don't need to chase your future
But you also shouldn't be afraid of it
Your fear should be
What you do in the meantime

There is no going back
I walk a very linear pathway
Through the threshold of each year
And even if I know what awaits me
I must try and hold my head high
And if I can't
I just won't buy a watch
Or stare at clocks
For as this thick broth settles
I breathe

Discontinued Rut

Wrong pipe, can't breathe
Decrease in lung capacity
I took a hit of the virus
I observed complacency
Injected the needle through my iris
Catalyzed the crisis
They want me to accept the scenery
But I don't really like this

It is a product they've designed
Inside, a corruption of the mind
I want to see beyond the drug
Before I resign to the prophet
Before the need to profit
I'm not living unconscious yet

Mindless masturbation
Who will audit this situation?
Who possesses complex introspection?
When skin is the depth of what we respect
There are dots we don't connect
And I'm no object
So I object to the pattern

I am trapped in a machine I didn't build
Where the idea died and truth was killed
And we are expected to swallow pills
To accept cheap thrills and submit
But I was promised more than this

I was given a vision
A glimpse through the bars of this prison
That with the abolition of addiction
We can be truly free
From the slavery of repetition
There is so much more that we are missing
There is so much left to find
But so many still live blind

Your Potential Hypothesis

What is the device of measurement?
What makes it evident?
This is just an estimate
My potential
What makes me so special?
Maybe I'm not capable
And what if greatness is overrated?
What if I become so good I become jaded?
What then?

Condemned if I don't follow your blueprint
You won't forgive me for being human
What if I don't want to be your student?
You will lead my happiness to ruin

You overwhelm me with expectation
Like sleeper cell activation
You push your hopes on me
I'm not responsible for your dreams
Nor will I ever be
A part of industrial society
I'm not just another cog piece

My potential is whatever I say it is
If I don't fulfill it
It's none of your business
My path is one I decide alone
I am more than a clone
More than clay for you to shape
I am a man who must find his own place
And learn to run at his own pace
Let me choose the dream I chase
And just be happy I found my own way

Disunity

At times we are caught up in self obsession
We have our own views and expectations
And it is a struggle to break away
We have rules we can't betray
So we remain loyal to ourselves

Empathizing with the enemy
Brings us closer to knowing balance
Steering us from entropy
And from becoming callous
Or else we are burdened by our selfishness
Perpetuating this poor precedent

This idea we seem to share
Where we all know what is best
So I caution to beware
Our truth is just a guess
And no perspective should be oppressed
Or viewed as innately false
If we do not show all sides respect
We will be at fault
Our morals tilt corrupt and fall

He who rejects his neighbor doesn't learn
So his story just repeats itself

Conjecture

To you my identity is:
A collection of your own assumptions
Based on observable details
And common social archetypes
You know my name, but you don't know the history
You see my face, but you don't know what it sees
So don't pretend for a moment you truly know me

You only know your limited perspective
which only demonstrates an inability
To be objective

I am no better but at least I know it
I don't pretend I comprehend
All of your complexities
I only sort them
Based on how they relate to me
But I try to understand
The rationale behind the things you do
The importance that it holds for you
And what your definition of important is

I will never claim I know you
I will never label what you are
I will never define your potential
But if you do these things to me
I will know you aren't trustworthy
And your words will lose all meaning

To presume to know the truth is arrogant
Assuming the answer contradicts intelligence
You are not credible
When you pull "facts" from behind a decimal
You only deceive yourself
And if you preach these conclusions
You deceive others as well

Growing Up

The child is the father of the man
I am a varied reflection of my younger self
Child me was the foundation of what I am today
We need to stop drawing the comparison
And start building a new foundation
Why do we haunt ourselves?
Am I just a ghost?
Made up of smaller parts
Fragments left over from another version
What is it that I originate?
Maybe it is not noteworthy
Maybe it is nothing at all
I am just the sum
Reiterated from another figure
Calculated over time
When do I stop living in my own shadow?
Or do I just embrace it?
Understanding that these building blocks
Have led me to where I stand
And will continue to push me forward

Futile Dream

Humans are imperfect creatures
Craving perfection desperately
Born with fear for the reaper
Time becomes our enemy

Every day death stalks us
And we feel the pressure rise
Can we complete our work on time?
No...
Completion is an illusion
We satisfy our initial needs
Then we invent some new ones

We are never content
Existing with a handicap
Drowning in greed we lament
The pursuit of perfection
Is the perfect trap

Forever cursed to chase our tails

Avoiding Vulnerability

When our words dance I feel like an outsider
Strapped into the social collider
Small talk ensues
I'll avoid making eye contact with you
Because your pupils will swallow me whole

I see myself inside them and am petrified
I am wearing a disguise
Afraid you're going to see through me
One, two, three
And the jig is up

You caught me in the act of being myself
But secretly wanting to be someone else
The pretender
Self-centered and self-censored
Trying desperately to keep you in the dark

The real me is overwhelming
But the buildup of lies has started swelling
And finally gave me away
How much does vulnerability weigh?
Because to me this shit is heavy

Inner fire

From the dust
Mother nature spun me into raw shapes
And I'm more than chemicals
But more than soul
A double helix tag
To mark the coming of the apes
The true beauty of drawing breath is all I know

As I stumble through this life
Until she calls my name
Age and an era change
Will signal an end to my journey
So as my fire dwindles down
I will stoke the embers flame
Because I'm not ready to go just yet
I'm still learning

I will cling to my beating heart
With sweaty shaking hands
Alive the dreamers fight
Until I prove I'm something special
The imagination
And the realization of a lifetime of plans
Be steadfast and hold strong
Until I rise to my potential

To at long last reach the top
Of my life's many rungs
And on that day
When my color fades into the grave
When my last breath crashes from out of my lungs
My inner fire will still be roaring strong ablaze

Perseverance

Summoning sunlight in the wake of storms
The parting clouds herald a new age
Blooming to an orchid the hydrangea transforms
But lost petals are preserved within a page
Remaining inside the last chapter I read
In this young book that continues on
Keeping track of all the ink that it has bled
Every old word an important icon
The basis, but not defining where this leads
So many pages ahead remain unknown
Each a chronicle of self-discovery
One that I will not undertake alone
For I am just one within the meadow
where the climate has been known to shift
And though we may adjust our tempo
Our rate of growth is ever swift
And if as one thing I made no headway
I will learn to take new form
Regardless of how well each chapter segues
Not one passage will be scorned

The Cycle

Solitary is my condition
And I am stubborn in my ways
My dreams are of ambition
But I dwell inside the cage
Of ice that bars my frozen soul
From ever taking form
But there is hope on the horizon
Shelter from the storm

The earth swallows and spits me out
Into the asphodel meadow
Where I take a number to join the ranks
Of the flower ghetto
And for many days we will grow
But still feel incomplete
Yearning to be transformed
And bloom with the coming heat

Harsh rays of sunlight
Will peel my wretched, dirty skin
Revealing to me the beautiful creature
That I hide within
So with every abandoned fragment
I engage in cleansing
And each time this event occurs
I find I am ascending

Soon I'll reach the climax
And be arrested by the breeze
Who with her winds will send my petals
To a burial at sea
The chillest cold will wither
And cause my bones to weaken
And I will die to be reborn
Next cycle of the seasons

Pull It Together

I feel broken
Like the translation is wrong
When my brain sends the signals
My voice butchers the language
And the right words are gone
Like a puzzle I can't solve
I can't find the pieces
Are they just lost?
Did they exist at all?

I am depressed
Had my head in the clouds
But when I got up there
Down came the storm
And every mountain I climb
I'm knocked down once more
Should I keep climbing?
Can I escape the downpour?

I'm conflicted
This heavy duality
My heart a dichotomy
I know what I want
But don't know what's good for me
With the decisions I make
Do I trust my impulses?
Or turn tail and flee?

Pull it together man
You've been down before
You'll be on your feet again
You have to be strong
Because if you learn more from losing
You've learned a lot
And if every defeat made you stronger
This cyclical pattern can't last much longer

Disenchantment

The well has run dry, but I thirst
I panic to refill the reservoir
But I can't understand the water bearer
For her tongue is enigmatic to me
Now suffering the drought
Fettered to a burning soma
I fantasize about the taste
Of the grand elixir ambrosia
And each droplet of nectar a miracle
Respiring into my lungs
Drawing the first breath
Of the new world

A sound breaks through my trance
The voice of the water bearer
She speaks sweetly,
"It is thirty silver to refill the well"
So I pay unto her my dues
And quaff the well dry again
The swill tastes of poison
And I vomit up black sludge
My thirst is not quenched
What vile brew have I consumed?
"Ambrosia", she smiles
Is it everything you hoped for?

Broken Projector

You are a projection
Born from the eclectic hive mind
Just another carbon copy
Just another you
From a long line of yous
Who seem to think you're special
But you're just a shell
Shaded in with stencils
Not real, but existential

I am a projection
Of my generation and society
And their proprietary claim
On individualism
We may be different colors
But refracted from the same prism
There is a defined limitation
On the sensation called ignorance
There is no meaning to our dissonance

We are all projections
But I have a confession
I am also the projector
The director and writer of the plot
With a few words I influence thought
And you react to me
Saving my mental data feed
Sharing my wisdom with friends
So they'll be less like them

And more like us

Because we are one
And every dream you'll ever have
Is someone else's rerun
Watched on a broken projector
And you'll replay it
Like a broken record

Preventive Measure

Mason of the clay
You only know how to shape blocks
Unimaginative and square
Stacking them one by one upwards
A wall to keep your enemies away
You call it a preventive measure

This is your defense
Justifying a lack of shapes so lazily
But I respect your ward
How hard you work to sustain it
Though I also pity you
How you barricade yourself into isolation

You are hidden from the outside world
Behind the artificial colossus
They know of you from hearsay
But have never seen your face
Unrecognizable to anyone
You are alone

Your wall may endure, but not you
You are not untouchable
Collapse this broken aegis
And in the rubble renewed
Take a new glance of the world
Beyond your comfort zone

Invalid By Proxy

We all want to achieve something
For ears of buzzing praise
Captives of the glory daze
We want acknowledgment now
Desperately trying to figure out
How to get it
But none are fit to give
Still we live our lives
Seeking validation
Through foreign eyes

I just want to be happy with myself
So when my life runs out
I won't have many regrets
And it doesn't have to be correct
Just acceptable
Everything we do is epochal
Changing within moments
Yet we tied our ropes to the locus
Of someone else's thoughts
It's time to untie these knots

Dire Disarmament

It's time to let go of all your ammo
A bullet without a firing chamber
Is a personal favor to yourself
Put your hatred on the shelf permanently
You are urgently in need of relief
A sheath exists for a meaningful purpose
Disarm all of your worthless weapons
Don't let them ever define who you are

Don't be beaten by inner demons
Obstacles strengthen you to find true peace
When achieved your problems will be distant
And you'll be a different person
The improved version you were meant to be
Cast your doubts into the sea and move on
Be someone you could count upon reliably
Undeniably you are all that holds you back

Addiction

I love you much like the liar loves the altruist
You are the only false deity to which I pray
And it seems I've become a master of burning bridges
You facilitate my need to get away
I'm gone and not coming back for days

I have no words to define this sensation
Anxiety addled brain cells power down
Synapses all come apart together
In this state of euphoria where I drown

I love you much like a killer loves his gun
Without it all I'd have is bloody fingers
You're the simply perfect tool for my trade
When I'm feeling blue you pull the trigger
And bring that rush of happy back in spades

I don't know what I'd do without you
Probably move on to bigger and better things
But you keep me safe inside your stasis
I'll never worry what tomorrow brings

I love you much like an astronomer loves the stars
For you I will stare down glass tubes for hours
Just to chart your odyssey through the sky
And given a single wish to make upon you
I will waste it on a trip with you tonight
I will waste it all just getting high

Pattern Shift

Have you ever wanted to change?
Dropping the many masks you adorn every day
To breathe new life into your lungs
And rekindle your spirit with a new flame
Emblazoned with a fresher paint

To reach a recidivism rate of zero
I will find that cancerous doubt
Dig deep and cut it out
The old ways are antiquated
Repetition is not optimal
It never was

Herald of the new era
Refugee of the chimera kingdom
Of a broken system
I flee and don't look back
The city is burning
And there is nothing left for me
So I won't be returning

Destruction as creation
The precursor to a change of direction
I will rebuild brick by brick
On the foundation of new ideas

Bright Side

If you can't be an optimist
You may need an optometrist
There is so much good to see
Even if your eyes are incompetent
Pessimist or realist
What is the difference?
Both aspire a negative influence
Focused on the darkness

Let the light shine through
Ignore your inclinations
Your worldview is askew
Built on uneven foundations
And thusly you cave to bias
Tipping over and one sided
A whole that has been divided

Negative is just a fraction
Derived through positive subtraction
You can choose which formula you use
Whether to be sad or laughing
Reacting to each moment passing by
If you can't be happy before you die
The least you can do is try
Looking on the bright side

Apple Tree Anarchy

Deep beneath the apple tree
In the crypt of my ancestors sits a statue
The statue compounds the sins of my forefathers
Towering above me, casting the longest shadow
It is my inheritance, but I reject it
I long to set fire to the effigy
To burn the apple tree to cinders
I can't, for I am the warden and the prisoner
I am bound by the helix cuffs
Like my mother, and her father before her
Like my father, and his mother before him
The consolidation of their woes
Another bastard born from wormwood

I will break down the paradigm
This apple will roll far away from the tree
Seeking to make roots in a greener forest
Where the seeds of a future generation
Will not be troubled by echoes of the old
Or the fractals of their disposition
Free from the genetic depression
Abandoning my inheritance
I will erect a new statue
And it will embody a new purpose
A symbol and a reminder
That we can forge our own paths in life
That an upbringing is an empty excuse

The Empathy Solution

Nothing ever gets better
When you only make it worse
Plucking quotes for the agenda
If he won't concede he'll be coerced
You can't claim to speak truth
When what you recite is rehearsed
You led the horse to water
When he said he doesn't thirst

It really doesn't matter
Who threw the stone first
Just that it was thrown
From the safety of a perch
Not so wealthy with empathy
You struggle to immerse
All you need to do is picture
Both your roles reversed

Momentarily

Staring out the window on this long drive
I observe the birds as they fly on the open sky
And rows of green trees
That give me a feeling I can't describe

This earth is alive for the moment
One day it will die and I know this
But sometimes I let myself forget
I get lost in my own head and pretend
That this story has no end
Though it is a lie
For the nature of all things is to die

The earth is no exception
This home is temporary
And everything that I see
Is a part of this limited session
That we call existence
Occurring over the span of a cosmic instance
So we must treasure our time dearly
And all the air we get to breathe
Before we cease to be

We are lucky to be here
To experience the beauty of this great sphere
Before it all disappears

Legacy

We aim to meet our goals in life
Every second we take in excess
Invites the possibility of death
The faster we work on our pyramid
The more likely it is be completed
And the longer we get to marvel
In the shadow of our accomplishment

I was born a sculptor in a world of stone
Born to a wild pack of builders
Very competitive in their art
But competition drives excellence
For only when we rise to a challenge
Do we discover our potential

My potential is still pending
But my clock is still ticking
At least for now

Will I rise or fall in my pursuit?
Can my chisel endure the breaking of bedrock?
Or is my swing too weak?

These are questions I will answer for myself
Over the course of my lifetime
As is tradition in my tribe
The fate of every builder
To be tested in this way

I will try my hands
And learn what I might produce
Before I die
So that my art may survive me

Pilgrimage

I prefer humanity over human race
Because I found no one wins
When all that matters is the value that I place
And while it may be influenced
The decision is one I make alone
This may all be just coincidence
But I'll turn over every stone
To find something that makes it worthwhile
And accept my path instead of counting miles

We're trying hard to make sense of our identities
There only is one single lock, but uncountable keys
We fumble through the pile looking for an answer
The time between filled by an exchange of banter

I can't find your answer friend
If you thought I had a clue, I don't
I'm just like you, I'm searching too
My cover has been blown
So return back to your search
You've got truth to find
But I'll still drop in on you
From time to time
And we can share every idea
Even if we find no panacea

The quest is on the contract
The one we signed at birth
To undergo this pilgrimage
To find out what we're worth
We won't stop until the day we die
We have truth to find

www.ingramcontent.com/pod-product-compliance
Lightning Source LLC
Chambersburg PA
CBHW081528040426
42447CB00013B/3377